5 Principles to a Purposeful Life

Larry Hawkins II

5 Principles to a Purposeful Life

Library of Congress Control Number: 2017919634
ISBN: 978-0-692-04740-8

Printed in the United States of America

Published by
Larry Hawkins II

Edited by
The Poised Professional, LLC

This book is dedicated to:

My wife, Trenay Hawkins:
My partner in this journey called life,
you stand beside me as we grow together,
you continually inspire me with your
greatness,
and you keep me accountable to my
purpose.
I love you.

My family, Larry Sr., Carol, and Nicole:
The foundation on which I stand,
you poured the concrete and held me up
until it dried. I carry you with me,
wherever I go.

My 42 influencers:
The words do not exist to properly
articulate how grateful I am to all of you.
This journey does not happen, without
your faith in me. Thank you.

ACKNOWLEDGEMENTS

Thank you to:

Dorothy Chamberlin & Carolyn Turner,
my praying grandmothers;

The HawkDG Team,
my partners in purpose;

Mia Hurley,
my awesome cover designer

Erin and Mary,
my magic creating editors

TABLE OF CONTENTS

5 Principles to a Purposeful Life

INTRODUCTION

SEVEN

For as long as I can remember, I've been fascinated with how things work. My dad, Larry Sr., occasionally tells a story that dates back to when I was seven years old. He had recently purchased a Tandy laptop, which at the time was a top of the line laptop, but it was cumbersome and required a bit of coordination to open. For a seven-year-old, opening it was seemingly impossible. There were latches on both sides that had to be held down simultaneously, and the monitor was extremely heavy.

From the moment my dad unboxed and turned it on, I was glued to his side. I watched him as he navigated Windows 3.1 and learned the ins and outs of the operating system. When he wasn't looking,

I would push a button on the keyboard just to see what would happen. For that entire week, any time he was operating the laptop, I was right there watching like a curious lab assistant. Eventually on Friday evening, I worked up the courage to ask dad if I could play with his new laptop by myself. He chuckled and replied, "If you can open it, you can play with it." The following morning, I knew exactly what I had to do.

If you grew up in the early '90s, then you know that a typical Saturday morning consisted of a huge bowl of cereal and the usual Saturday morning cartoon lineup. However, when my mom woke up this particular Saturday morning and walked into the living room, she didn't find me happily watching cartoons. Instead, she walked in the living room and immediately yelled, "BOY WHAT ARE YOU DOING?! LARRY, WAKE UP AND GET IN HERE!" My dad jumped out of bed and raced into the living room to see what was wrong.

Naturally, he was expecting the worst. He frantically asked, "What's wrong!?" My mom replied, "That child of yours is on your expensive new laptop!" I sat on the floor terrified because I didn't know what I did wrong. I had been quietly playing solitaire and suddenly there was commotion in the living room. Dad looked at me, looked at my mom, and finally burst out laughing. He eventually caught his breath and said, "Well, I told him if he could open it, he could play with it." He laughed again and went back to bed with the biggest smile on his face. If you ask my dad, he'll tell you that this was the moment he knew I was destined for greatness. For me, that was the moment I knew I wanted to learn as much as I could about how electronics worked.

SIXTEEN

At the age of sixteen, I obtained one of my crowning achievements—I was finally taller than my dad. I used to sneak up behind him, shine his head, and tell him to be still so I could see my reflection. Turning sixteen was also pivotal for me because I had been accepted into the Mississippi School for Math and Science (MSMS) in Columbus, MS. MSMS is one of the premier schools in the state of Mississippi. It's a college-prep high school where the best and the brightest in the state live on a college campus for their final two years of high school. Being accepted meant that I would leave all the comforts of my home in Pascagoula, MS and live four hours away. I had never been more excited.

As the day grew closer for me to depart, my dad sat me down because he wanted to have a serious, heartfelt conversation. He said to me: "Son, I want you to know that I'm extremely proud of you. The grades that you've made, and the people that you've helped, I couldn't be prouder. But, where you're going, no one knows what you've done and frankly, no one cares." I didn't know what to make of his words, so I had this look of confusion on my face and replied, "Thank……you….?" He said to me, "I tell you this because when you leave this house, it is fully up to

you to decide who you are going to be,

what people are going to associate with

you, and how you're going to make an

impact on the lives of the people that you

meet. And, I have full confidence in you

because you have everything you need to

be successful." He went on to say, "I have

this confidence because we raised you with

core values, those things inside of you that

keep you centered. What you do with

those core values, how you put them into

action, those are your principles. Principles

are fundamental truths that guide your actions because they are ingrained in who you are. Your principles are the number one thing that determine your life progress." These were his parting words as I left home, and they've stuck with me ever since.

As I left to go pursue a high school diploma, degrees, internships, my first full-time job, and ultimately found Hawkins Development Group, I realized how right he was. Every single thing that you touch, everything you create, every person that you interact with, and everything you do will find your principles ingrained in it. When I left home, my principles were not fully defined but over time my life experiences helped me refine the principles that would come to define me as a person.

Ultimately, these five principles have guided me on my journey to pursue my life's purpose. It is this pursuit that has led me to write this book. My hope is that by telling my story and covering the lessons

I've learned, I can share at least one thing that will help you on your journey. The principles of motivation, purpose, betterment, contribution, and mastery changed my life; hopefully, they can change yours too.

PRINCIPLE #1: MOTIVATION

"Always question your motivations,
because every action that you take ties
back to your motivation."
– Larry Hawkins II

May 2011 – Graduation Day at Mississippi State University

5 Principles to a Purposeful Life

TRUE LOVE

My entire college career, from my major to extracurricular organizations and graduation date, was a series of choices due to my motivations. It was during this six-year period that I came to understand the power of questioning your motivations. Yes, you read that right, it took me SIX years to graduate. But we'll get to that soon enough.

Going all the way back to when I was seven years old and I opened that Tandy laptop, I knew I wanted to work with computers. After graduating high school, I still had a passion for computers and figuring out how things worked. When I entered college, it seemed natural for me to major in computer engineering. My goal was not to have the highest GPA, but instead, to have the most well-rounded experience. With this in mind, I wanted to be as involved as possible with campus organizations.

At the time my two motivators, computers and campus involvement, were often at odds. For a freshman, adjusting to college is a crash course on time management. You quickly learn that instructors give homework as if their class is the only one on your schedule. When this is the standard practice across four to six different classes, plus lab work, free time becomes scarce. Then to add in campus organizational responsibilities, I felt like I had more plates to spin than available hands, but I started spinning them as best I could.

Because I had enough college credits to join a fraternity my freshman year, I was initiated into the Kappa Beta chapter of Alpha Phi Alpha, Fraternity, Inc. This immediately put a strain on my academics because my extracurricular activities seemed to take priority over computer engineering. The week after my initiation, our chapter hosted our annual "Alpha Week," which was full of service activities.

Because this occurred in November, I was already swamped with homework and lab assignments as professors prepared us for final exams.

I distinctly remember having a time conflict between a computer engineering lab and a fraternity event. This was the first event since my initiation where I'd be able to get involved with the community. I figured since I was only missing one lab, I could make up my grade with the other ones. I was so excited about engaging with the fraternity because service to the community was why I joined. I ended up skipping the lab and making a zero on the assignment that day.

As the semester progressed, I continued to grapple with focusing on grades or spending time with my fraternity brothers. More often than not, I chose the latter, which led to a "C" in my computer programming course. My teacher noted that my lab absence was the deciding factor between a C and a B.

That semester, I was often engaged in community service activities through my work in the fraternity. However, I had one of the lowest GPAs of my entire college career, because I hadn't learned how to balance things yet. At the time I thought this was just irresponsibility on my end, but I can look back and acknowledge that it happened because my work with my fraternity got me closer to my true love: helping other people.

THE SIX-YEAR DEGREE

My freshman year of college reinforced that computer engineering was at odds with my love for helping people. While I still loved computers and electronics, the realities of computer engineering meant that I spent more time with computers than I did people. I loved interacting with people more, which led to me switching my major to electrical engineering. From my conversations with my advisor, this major would afford me more opportunities to be in people-focused roles due to the major's flexibility. Already, I was learning to balance my various motivations to take actions that would better align me with my purpose. I just didn't know it.

As the years progressed, I got more involved with campus, specifically in organizations that would engage me with people: I became a senior Resident Assistant in Residence Life, chapter president for my fraternity, and treasurer for my local chapter of National Society for

Black Engineers. Academically, I still had many unanswered questions about how my major translated into the real world.

Thankfully, my university offered a cooperative education (co-op) program. Participating in this program involved completing at least three alternating semester-long internships at an affiliated company. This program provided real world experience in my major, at the expense of extending my time in school.

After completing my first internship rotation, I met with my advisor to determine if I was on track to graduate in four years. My advisor had bad news: I could only graduate on time if I skipped the last co-op semester. This would mean that I would not complete the cooperative education program and miss out on valuable work experience. I still had unanswered questions about my major, there were still things I wanted to do with my campus organizations, and I still felt I had more to learn about myself as a person. As I analyzed my decision, I accepted that foregoing my final co-op rotations would accelerate my graduation time.

However, one of my first motivations coming into college was to leave a well-rounded student, which included good grades and community involvement as well as extensive work experience. These things would adequately prepare me to be more involved with others, no matter where I worked. I made the decision to extend my time in school and make the most of my extra time. I went on to complete four internships, which proved to be invaluable when it came time to interview for employment. This leads me to the third key moment in which my motivations helped me make the right decision.

Before making the decision to extend my time in college, I was originally on track to graduate May 2009. Unknown at the time, that would prove to be a difficult time to enter the job market due to the economy. Following my motivations

opened doors in the form of two lucrative

job offers; the first offer came from Procter

& Gamble (P&G) and the second offer

came from National Instruments (NI). I

originally interviewed with NI in 2009 and

stayed in contact with them over the years.

August 2010, I was accepted into P&G's

Top Engineering Talent Recruiting Event

(TETRE) where I was one of twenty

people, out of two thousand nationwide

applicants, invited to visit and interview for

a job with the company. During my

interview, one of the interviewers noted that one of the most impressive things on my resume was my extensive work experience. My decision to follow my motivations and complete more internship rotations was paying off in real-time.

As you progress on your journey, you're going to find yourself competing with other people for some of the same opportunities, and it's the small decisions you make that will separate you from other people. Because I decided to stay in school an extra semester to finish my co-op program, it set me on a path to leave the TETRE program with a job offer in hand in 2010. I thought that this decision to extend my time at Mississippi State was going to be the hardest motivation-based decision I would have to make. Boy, was I wrong.

RUBBER MEETS ROAD

October 2010, I flew to Austin, TX to interview with NI for an opportunity to join their Engineering Leadership Program (ELP). This was a twelve to eighteen month program where participants learned about the company and were offered additional leadership development opportunities. From the moment I walked onto the department's floor, I knew this place was special. Everywhere I looked, I saw engineers who were fresh out of college working on various projects and solving engineering challenges. What made this department stand out is that they were collaborating with other engineers and having fun while doing it. Some of them were on phone calls talking to customers, some were working together to piece together a circuit, and others were gathered around a computer screen writing computer code as a team. It was as if my love for engineering and passion for helping people collided.

After interviewing and returning home, I was extended an offer. I was at the crossroad of where I would start my full-time career. This was going to be a huge, life-changing decision. P&G was going to pay me significantly more to do focused engineering work in a production plant environment; NI was going to pay me less, but I would still be working in engineering while engaging with others.

This situation was the culmination of all of the previous decisions that I had made to this point. Should I follow the money or should I follow my passion? Even though most people may have chosen the job that paid more, my motivations were centered on how I could do engineering and also impact people. My college career was built on this, and I wanted to be sure to continue this as I entered the workforce. I ultimately chose the position at NI, and although it paid less, it seemed to be more fulfilling. The magnitude of this decision would not be revealed for another few years. For now, I was confident in what I learned about my motivations, how they

impact my actions, and the importance of

keeping them aligned at all times. The

fruits of this phase of my journey are

directly tied to the principle of motivation.

KNOWLEDGE OF SELF

In every situation we're in, we have an ideal outcome. From a psychological standpoint, our motivations are the beginning of us reaching that ideal outcome. Take a couple moments and make a list of every single thing that motivates you.

Got it?

Good.

It is important to understand what motivates us because our motivations affect our desires. Let's use a common motivator that we can all relate to—hunger. Hunger is a basic, physiological motivator according to Maslow's Hierarchy of Needs. Abraham Maslow used the terms physiological, safety, belongingness/love, esteem, and self-actualization to describe the needs and the patterns through which human motivations generally move.

Understanding Maslow's hierarchy is vital to understanding the first principle because it shapes how motivation applies to your life. It is important to note, the principle of motivation is applied from a place of stability where your existing needs (i.e. food, shelter, love, etc.) are being met. It is from this place of stability that we can see how various motivations can combine to impact our decisions.

Imagine that you're sitting on the couch, watching TV, and your stomach rumbles. You know that means you're hungry, so you now go from desiring to watch TV, to desiring to eat food. Well, if your motivations affect your desires, your desires affect your priorities. Again, you're sitting on the couch watching TV; you're now hungry and desire food, and consequently you have to re-prioritize what you plan to do for the next ten minutes to solve this problem of hunger. Nothing here is groundbreaking.

If motivations affect our desires, and desires affect priorities, then our priorities affect our choices. Maslow's theory on the human hierarchy of needs, specifically on multiple motivations of behavior, highlights that we are simultaneously motivated by different things at different levels.

We've established you're motivated by hunger, but imagine you're also motivated by a desire to lose weight to fit in your favorite jeans. This would trace back to the "esteem" level of Maslow's theory. Not only do you have to re-prioritize your time, but you also have to choose your food option based on these motivators. So what does this look like in real-time?

You're sitting on the couch, you're hungry, you prioritize getting off of the couch and walking over to the fridge, over watching the rest of your TV show. While you're standing at the fridge, you have two options: one healthy, one unhealthy. If you're just motivated by hunger, you can eat anything. In this case, you're motivated by hunger and a desire to lose weight, so you choose the apple over the burger.

You've gone from sitting on the couch, watching your favorite TV show, to standing in the kitchen eating a healthy apple all because of your motivations. This is so basic that you don't think twice about it, but psychologically speaking, there is a lot going on for an entire exchange that took two minutes or less.

This happens with every decision from deciding what to eat to selecting life-defining opportunities. With this new knowledge, what lessons are there to be gained? More importantly, what are the potential pitfalls?

I'm glad that you asked.

PRODUCER VS. CONSUMER

I chose the position at National Instruments because I saw myself as an engineer who engaged with people. The job involved providing technical support to other professors, engineers, and scientists that were using NI's products. Soon after I started, I had the opportunity to meet the leader of the services and support organization in which ELP belonged. During this meeting, he issued a challenge to everyone in the room. He challenged us to set goals for ourselves that would allow us to make a meaningful difference for the department. He challenged us to find ways to be better versions of ourselves by making an impact on everything we touched.

He closed his sentiments by emphasizing that the path to making a difference started with ourselves. I felt like he was talking directly to me the entire time, and that shaped my approach to the role. Years later, I found out that he *was* talking directly to me, and we've been good friends ever since.

My first priority was mastery over my role because I couldn't help someone else if I couldn't do my own job. I became so well versed in technical support that I would often finish all of my work early. I could have easily gone home early, but I chose to stay late and help my peers. I chose to share my knowledge with those around me. Although I loved engineering, I was more motivated by helping people.

Understanding my motivations allowed me to immediately make a positive impact not only in my job, but also with my peers. It was this same motivation that led the department manager's speech to resonate with me so strongly. Because of these same motivations, I entered the department looking for ways to use my talents to produce for others. This led to me achieving awards and promotions faster than the department average. The awards and promotions were not as important as what it afforded me—more opportunities to help people. The lesson that I learned was that understanding my motivations is only the beginning. The value of this principle comes to life when you're able to apply your motivations to produce for the benefit of others.

The other side of the producer vs. consumer battle is deciding to use the motivations for self. Following this path leads to becoming a victim of consumerism. When you're in school, you're a consumer. You show up at school, sit in your desk, and consume everything that you're given, told, shown, etc. The extent of your production involves homework, taking tests, and the occasional project; these tasks are more like regurgitating what's been consumed rather than producing something new.

College is more of the same. You go from class to class thinking, "*What's in it for me?*" The problem with this is that many times people carry this mindset into the workplace. Your priorities are *"What can I do to get a bigger raise?"*, *"What can I do to get the next award?"*, or *"What can I do to make myself look better?"* All of these questions are rooted in consumerism.

A mentor from NI told me, "The quickest way to stand out from your peers is to go from consumer to producer." It wasn't until I was able to understand this perspective that I fully understood what he meant.

Use your talents and motivations to identify how you can add value to your family, your peers, and even your employer. This shift in mindset will not only make you stand out, but it will also enable you to better understand how to improve as a person and make you even more valuable.

5 Principles to a Purposeful Life

PRINCIPLE #2: PURPOSE

"We each have a unique purpose, a calling that we're obligated to discover." – Larry Hawkins II

July 2014 – The day HawkDG shirts arrived

5 Principles to a Purposeful Life

BOOM

There was a husband and father who was tormented by inner demons, so he turned to alcohol to numb the pain. When he was sober, he was the nicest man you could ever meet and would give you the shirt off his back. When he was intoxicated, he was mean and angry.

It was this same anger that carried him home one day. His wife and kids were home when he walked in the door, and that's when things took a turn for the worse. It wasn't long before he attacked his wife, releasing all of his anger. This wasn't the first time this happened, and the man's oldest son had seen enough.

Although only nine years old, the son had been witness to a lifetime of abuse and it hurt him to see his mother in such pain. He did the only thing he felt that he could and ran to find the family's shotgun. It all happened so quickly: the man hit his wife, the son grabbed the gun, the man hit his wife again, the son aimed at his father, the man hit his wife a third time, and the son pulled the trigger.

Click.

The shotgun, fully loaded and in perfect condition, misfired. The man looked up and channeled his rage into attacking his son. In that moment, the son had protected his mother and shouldered the load for his family. Soon after, the mom gathered her kids and left her husband for good.

The troubled father in this story was my biological grandfather. The son who protected his mother was my father. I

almost never wrote this book. Not because

I was afraid, but because I almost never

existed. If that gun didn't misfire, my dad

would have killed my grandfather and gone

to jail. He never would have met my mom

or had me. That's the fragility of purpose.

In the blink of an eye, many lives could

have been destroyed. However, many

lives have been positively impacted since

that day.

ONE MORE SIP

There was a son and a friend tormented by his inner demons, so he turned to alcohol to numb the pain. When he was sober, he was the nicest guy you could ever meet, and would give you the shirt off his back. When he was intoxicated, he was mischievous and reckless.

It was this same recklessness that that carried him downstairs one night to host a party. His friends were there when he came downstairs and that's when things took an unexpected turn. He met a young lady who captured his attention, and he lived the next few months with little regard for academic or personal responsibility.

Although only twenty-two years old, he had been witness to what felt like a lifetime of abuse, and it hurt him to see himself in such pain. He did the only thing he felt that he could and found the closest bottle. It all happened so quickly: the man took a drink, the young lady grabbed his attention, the man failed a test, the young lady grabbed his hand, the man almost failed the semester, but the young lady grabbed his heart.

Love.

The young man who had fallen so low that he needed counseling to stay afloat had rediscovered meaning in his path. In that moment, the young lady protected the man from himself and shouldered the load for his family. Soon after, the young man gathered himself and resumed pursuing his purpose.

That troubled young man in this story was me. The life-saving young lady is my wife. I almost never wrote this book. Not because I was afraid, but because I almost fell victim to alcoholism and the demons of my past. If I had taken one more sip, I would have failed that semester. If I had failed that semester, I would have been ineligible to continue with my co-op, and who knows where I would be.

Again, this is the fragility of purpose.

In the blink of an eye, many lives could

have been destroyed. However, many

lives have been positively impacted since

that day.

PURPOSE TAKES ROOT

There was a husband and friend, who was inspired by his passions, so he searched for any opportunity to share his gift. When he was engaged, he was the most focused man you could ever meet and would sacrifice his own for others. When he was disinterested, he searched for ways to hone his skills for the greater good.

It was this same passion that led him to a role as a leader of his peers in the workplace. When he inherited a team that wasn't motivated, he felt driven to turn things around. That team of sixteen engineers started to believe in themselves.

Although only twenty-five years old, his face lit up when motivating others; the joy he felt seeing others focused on their goals was unmatched. His passion and joy led to him creating something that would forever change his life. It all happened so quickly: the man taught his class, the team bought into the vision, the man coached his team members, the team started to excel, the man set higher goals, and the team broke department records.

Purpose.

The man had finally discovered his calling, his reason for existing. In that moment, the man stood ready for the world and ready to shoulder the load for others. Soon after, the man was given the opportunity to spread his message to others and follow his purpose forward.

I was that twenty-five year-old man, and that man is still a part of me. I wrote this book because I felt compelled to share my principles with others. The path of purpose is fragile, the path of purpose is difficult, but the path of purpose is rewarding.

If you're reading this book, I'm sure there have been moments in your life that could have gone a different way, but they didn't. You owe it to those moments and those who will be impacted by your journey to pursue your purpose and make

a meaningful impact.

PASSION IS NOT PURPOSE

Imagine that you wake up in the middle of the night sweating. You look over to the window and discover that your curtains are missing. You look at the wall and see that the paint is peeling. You walk into the kitchen and see a pot of boiling water. Which of these problems do you fix first?

You put out the fire.

The fire is causing you to sweat, burned your curtains, peeled the paint off the wall, and forced the water to boil. You put out the fire because it's the *root problem* that needs to be solved. Finding your life's purpose is much like this riddle.

This analogy is important because pursuing our passions and finding the common themes between them is the key to finding purpose. The reason that we're able to identify that the fire exists is because we're able to look for commonalities between the various events. The way that you're able to identify your purpose is by looking for commonalities between your various passions.

It's important to remember that purpose shows up differently in each of us. A person's purpose may be preventing suicide in people with depression, decreasing illiteracy in impoverished areas, creating technology to revolutionize the way we communicate, or inspiring others to pursue their dreams.

For example, there are many ways to manifest the passion of suicide prevention in people with depression. It could show up as passion for helping others in general, a passion for mental health, a passion for being a good listener, a passion for solving problems, or a passion for wanting people to feel included.

This same combination of passions could manifest in a variety of ways across a variety of professions and disciplines, but it's important to understand why they're important to you. Someone who is fascinated with the chemistry of the brain would relate to those passions differently than someone who had a family member who was dealing with a mental illness.

Understanding your past is equally important as your current interest. It's your responsibility to engage with life and explore your passions to see where the journey leads.

I truly, honestly, and fundamentally believe that everyone is on earth for a purpose—this concept is not something that is reserved for only the special few. It also is not something to take lightly because finding purpose is a heavy responsibility. We each have something inside of us to provide to the greater good, and we have an obligation to discover it. Finding purpose in your life is as much about the journey itself as it is the destination. Passion is not purpose, but it is the sign that you're moving in the right direction.

THE PURSUIT OF HAPPINESS

I'm frequently asked "How did you go from engineering to public speaking?" My response is always the same: pursuing my passions. I opened this book with this line for a reason, "*For as long as I can remember, I've been fascinated with how things work.*" That one sentence summarizes my path of pursuing my passions.

It all started with my fascination for my dad's laptop, and moved to handheld video games, remotes, alarm clocks, and

my sister's toys—all of which I took apart

and reassembled with varying degrees of

success. I also made it a point to better

understand my peers, teammates, friends,

girlfriends, and mentors to identify the best

way to communicate with them.

Whether it was an electronic device

or a person, I was fascinated with how it

worked. It was this innate curiosity that

followed me across the different stages

into adulthood that led to my major, place

of employment, and the founding of my business. Where my passions went, I closely followed. The manifestation of this book is no different. The biggest lesson that I learned when it came to applying this principle to my life was to pursue opportunities that align with your passion and just follow the path as it twists and turns.

You can think of passion in terms of what types of activities would you pay money to do? If you're willing to make a personal sacrifice, whether it's time,

money, or inconvenience, then you're

moving towards passion. However, that is

often easier said than done. It's in those

moments that I then turn to Oprah

Winfrey's quote,

> *"Knowing what you don't want to do is the best possible place to be if you don't know what to do, because knowing what you don't want to do leads you to figure out what it is you really want."*

If you find trouble identifying what

you're passionate about, start with

identifying things you've tried that you

don't enjoy. Work to understand

specifically what made it unpleasant, and

then use this information when you begin

searching for something new.

WHAT PURPOSE IS NOT

One of the common misconceptions about pursuing purpose is that it has to be a full-time job to be worthy of pursuit. This is absolutely false. In a recent workshop I taught, we completed an exercise on finding purpose and a participant asked, "What do I do if I find my purpose has nothing to do with my job?" As I prepared to answer the question, another participant provided the correct answer, "That's perfectly okay. That just means that your job provides you stability to allow you to pursue your purpose in your personal time."

Sure, we would all love to get paid to pursue purpose, but there is no requirement that states your purpose must pay your bills. Some of the richest people in the world found their true passions in their philanthropic efforts. Of course, the closer we're able to align our "day job" with what lights our soul on fire, the more rewarding our pursuit of happiness becomes, but a passion isn't less significant because it doesn't align with a career.

As you search for your passions, and ultimately your purpose, one thing to be wary of is centering your passion around your skills just because you've been told you're good at something. Think of how often you've found yourself doing something because everyone in the office knew you were good at that particular task. What started as you being helpful soon became "other duties as assigned."

The danger here is that when you start looking for passions to explore, you will naturally start with your talents. This is harmless, but when pigeonholed into a task based on proficiency rather than passion, you are setting yourself up for dissatisfaction in the long run.

See the following chart. Activities you don't enjoy doing, and you're not good at are labeled as "painful." The intersection of activities you don't like doing, but you're good at are considered "chores." The intersection of activities you like doing, but you're not good are "hobbies." Lastly, the intersection of activities you like doing, and you're equally good at are described as "passions."

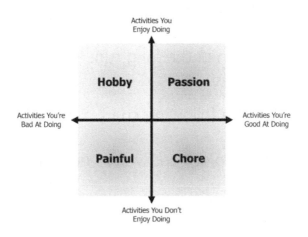

Activities and tasks that fall into the "hobby" category are great for relaxation and self-care, which will help reenergize you on your quest for purpose; however, the ultimate goal is to locate activities and tasks that fall into this "passion" category that lead to purpose.

5 Principles to a Purposeful Life

PRINCIPLE #3: BETTERMENT

"Always leave others better off than before they met you." – Larry Hawkins, Sr.

1999 – Family picture before church

GIVE

I only have one biological sibling, but my mother nurtured seven additional children. That turned me into a jealous son, and I wouldn't change a thing.

In many denominations of the Christian faith, there's a concept of the godparent. Godparents bear witness to another child's baptism and assume a vested interest in the life and upbringing of that child. Those godparents help the godchild's family by providing for the godchild when they can, and in some cases spending time with them throughout the span of the child's life. Most families don't have many godchildren—my mom has seven.

This turned me into a jealous son because this meant that I had to share. For the stereotypical godparent, they would send gifts at major holidays and maybe babysit their godchild once every few months. Not only did I have to share my mom, but I also had to share my food, toys, TV time, and sometimes even my bed what felt like every weekend. Sure, I already had to share some of these things with my sister, but this was different. In my mind, these other people weren't my blood relatives, so why did I have to share with them?

Each of her godchildren had different backgrounds and different levels of needs. Because of my jealousy, I watched my mom's interactions with her godchildren with extreme attentiveness, and soon I started to understand. The dynamic of a godparent-godchild wasn't about what you had to give up, it was about how you were able to help meet their needs. Being a godmother did not take away my mother's love for me.

Because she had so much love to give, she was able to give her godchildren love and attention that they needed at that point in their life. My mom taught me that giving was about doing for others what they couldn't do for themselves simply because you can and it's the right thing to

do.

LOVE FOR ALL MANKIND

One of the highlights of my college career was my time as president of the Kappa Beta Chapter of Alpha Phi Alpha Fraternity, Inc. The aims of Alpha Phi Alpha Fraternity, Inc. are manly deeds, scholarship, and love for all mankind. Those aims attracted me to the fraternity, as well as shaped my approach to my position as president. The love for all mankind reminded me a lot of my parents, and how they raised me to help others.

One day, I had an idea for our chapter to adopt a family in need. We contacted the local Salvation Army and they connected us with a family of four in need. The father was unemployed and looking for a job. The mother had a job, and the son and daughter were in need of clothes for school. Honestly, this was a task that was beyond the scope of what we were prepared to do, which made it simultaneously rewarding and draining.

We spent the next few months hosting fundraisers, purchasing gas, food, clothing, and providing transportation for the father to get to job interviews. Because we as fraternity members shouldered this responsibility in addition to our academic loads, we quickly became experts in communication and collaboration. The family had two points of contact with our chapter: me and the vice-president.

Anytime they had a need, they would contact us and then we would have to decide the best course of action to meet their needs. Sometimes it was communicating that we were unable to provide assistance, and other times it was sending out mass text messages to see who could best meet their need. Anyone can say they have love for all mankind, but true impact is made through living it.

We exhausted our budget for helping this family, and I eventually contacted my dad for financial help when the family was in a bind. I knew that we could replenish our funds with time, but this family did not have such a luxury. With time, we were able to help the family get back on their feet, and no longer in need of our assistance. This was another reminder that giving was about doing for others what they couldn't do for themselves.

PEOPLE ENGINEERING

April 2012, ten months after I started working at NI, I applied for and received the newly created role of Core Team Manager for the ELP department. One of the notable reasons that I received the role was because of my work as a team leader and former mentor in my short time in the department. I was being rewarded for the fruit that I produced. In this role, my sole responsibility was the onboarding and development of the department's new hires. The transition to this role was significant because I would be moving

completely away from engineering work

and focusing solely on professional

development of new engineers. For

someone who spent six years securing a

degree in electrical engineering, making a

conscious decision to pursue a role not

directly relating to engineering required

significant sacrifice. This was my

opportunity to take my passions and make

a direct impact on the future of the

department.

Because the role was new, there was a lot of work to be done to ensure its success. I inherited a skeleton of the twelve-week program and built it from there. I had now gone from software programming and analyzing circuits, to designing training and analyzing performance metrics.

Through my experience in previous leadership roles, I knew that sustainable success was bigger than one person. One of my first priorities was creating new mentor and team leader roles within the scope of the program that would prepare current members of the department for future leadership roles.

In my role I found ways to help people become better versions of themselves and prepare them for their future. Over the course of the fifteen months that I served in this role, I oversaw the development of ninety-four new hires and thirty-seven mentors; as a result, there was an increase in key performance

indicators up to five hundred percent.

Every moment that was devoted to

the improvement of the onboarding

program was another example of

sacrificing to provide others with what they

needed to be successful. Now, let's explore

what this principle means for you.

YOUR INNER ENTREPRENEUR

Let's start with a simple fact: you are the CEO of your own business. You are in the business of you—You, Inc. You are a seller, offering your skills, traits, abilities, and services to others. When in the business of YOU, every interaction is a transaction.

Remember that time you held the door open for the family as they walked in to the store? Yeah, that was a transaction. Do you remember the big project that you executed flawlessly for your boss? Yep, that's another transaction. Remember all those nights you checked under your child's bed for the boogeyman? That was a transaction, too.

Every single interaction you have with every person that you come in contact with is a transaction. Transactions imply an exchange of currency, and these situations are no different. In the business of you, your currency comes in three different forms: time, trust, and opportunities.

Time is our most precious resource, as we have a finite amount of it. Imagine that you go to a movie that ends up being terrible. The moment you walk out of the theater, what is your first thought?

"That was a waste of my time."

Why is that our first reaction? When something wastes our time, our first thought is of the many other things we could have done with that same amount of time. A similar occurrence happens when we work with someone else and, due to their efforts, the outcome does not meet our expectations. In fact, having our time wasted by someone else has a larger impact on our views on the value of time. Making an intentional decision to place your time in someone else's hands is one of the most important, and most common, examples of social transactions. This is important because being intentional with our usage of our time directly impacts the next form of currency—trust.

The more time spent with someone, the more you two begin to trust each other. Trust increases if the time is spent in a way that meets everyone's expectations. How much trust do you place in someone that you've never worked with? Probably

not much because you two haven't gotten

to know each other. Time can affect

whether trust increases or decreases.

If every interaction with a coworker

is a disappointment, trust decreases.

Likewise, if every interaction is positive,

trust increases.

If your goal is to leave every person

better off than before you met them, then

you're doing your part to ensure most, if

not all, interactions are positive. When

sufficient trust has been built amongst your

sphere of influence, this unlocks the third form of currency—opportunities.

When you take care of other people's time and leave them better off than before they met you, their trust in you increases. When their trust in you increases, they're more likely to recommend you for opportunities. Think of how often you've recommended a friend for a job opportunity or had someone offer you the opportunity to network with a person of interest. These types of occurrences are so common to our lives that we don't think much about them. However, when we examine them in detail, we see that we've been in the business of "us" since birth. Now that we're aware of the rules of engagement, let's examine how we can leverage this information more intentionally.

INVESTING FOR THE FUTURE

I'm in the business of inspiring others to pursue purpose. As such, I treat every person I come in contact with like a potential customer. Every interaction that we have aligns with my mission of helping other people because ultimately that is the service I provide. Following this approach enables me to be confident that I'm giving each person the very best of me at all times, no matter how small, or large, the interaction.

Back before the idea of Hawkins Development Group existed, I was teaching my career development course free of charge around NI. My primary motivation for doing this was because I knew I created something that could help people, and I wanted to take every advantage to do that. August of 2013 found me at the beginning stages of this companywide teaching journey.

In this particular class, there was a young lady who was very unhappy with her current role and future career prospects.

She completed the course and went on to apply the teachings to her life. A couple years later, after Hawkins Development Group had been formed, I started following up with various class attendees to learn how their career had changed since completing the course. Sitting down with this young lady was an eye-opener.

As she recalled how unmotivated and burned out she was in her job at the time, I eagerly waited to hear whether I helped her at all. She shared with me that by completing the course, and having an accountability partner, she was able to make a significant change in her career. At the time of our interview, she was extremely happy in her new role and attributed the transition to the course's teachings. I was overjoyed to see that I was able to make a tangible impact.

To close our interview, I asked her if she knew of anyone who could potentially benefit from the course's teachings. She replied that her mom was a director at a different company, and she would recommend me to her. What happened next exceeded all of my expectations. She introduced me to her mother as, "Mom, this is the guy who changed my life."

It was in that moment that the principle of betterment came full circle. Solely because I was finding ways to share my passion and purpose with people, I was able to make a significant impact on someone's life. Her mom went on to introduce me to the training manager at her company, and this company went on to become one of our biggest clients.

You have to approach EVERY interaction with the utmost care because you understand the value of time, trust, and opportunities. Doing good for the sake of doing good has high actual and intrinsic value.

Doing good will bring more opportunities to impact more people with your passions and your purpose. To reach this stage, you have to make the most of every interaction and always strive to leave others better off than before they met you.

SELF-CARE

In the spring of 2008, I was chapter president, step-captain, and intake coordinator for my fraternity, senior Resident Assistant of my dormitory, and member of the alpha class for the Appalachian Leadership Honors Program. In addition, I had strained relationships with both my girlfriend and my parents—all while taking sixteen hours worth of classes. Coincidentally, the spring of 2008 is where I learned about the danger of neglecting yourself while walking your journey. Every single day of that semester was a fight for my sanity, while doing my best to not let others down. It's very easy to spend so much time focused on others that you never stop to think about what you want.

There were days where I would leave my room at 7:55 a.m. to race to my 8:00 a.m. class, and return after 2:00 a.m. This became the norm for me—a constant blur of classes, labs, study groups, step practice, community service, tests, arguments with my girlfriend, missed appointments, traveling to perform in shows, and conference meetings with the residents in my residence hall. Every now and then, I would find time to eat or sleep.

Eventually, I became so stressed that I was lashing out at my friends and ignoring my girlfriend and parents altogether. Frankly, I was too stressed to even get out of the bed. I hit rock bottom.

That semester gave literal meaning to the quote, "*You cannot serve from an empty vessel,*" by Eleanor Brownn. With time, I realized the only way I would make it through the semester was by delegating responsibilities and learning to say no. I had lost track of who I was as an individual because I had given my all to everyone else. It's the thought of making this mistake again, or seeing someone else make this mistake, that makes me such a strong supporter of practicing self-care.

I've asked many people "What is it that *you* want to do?" Many times, they are taken aback by this question. They're surprised because they've lived life always fulfilling their responsibilities to their spouse, children, coworkers, boss, or community that they no longer know what they want. They exist to serve others and nothing else. When they ask where they should start to figure it out, I always recommend finding something that is just for them.

Some people enjoy blogging, knitting, painting, playing video games, or reading. For me, I love lifting weights. I've found that the discipline required to consistently lift weights and gain muscle translates very easily to my life outside the gym. That same discipline aids me in serving others while not neglecting myself.

Lifting weights energizes me and has

become one of my true passions.

Understanding where your passions lay is

important because just as it can lead you

to purpose. It also allows you to tap into

that internal source of energy and

excitement when things get tough.

Increasing your knowledge in what

drives you, and then allowing that to be

the guide in your interactions with other

people is how you apply this principle to

your daily interactions. This principle

emphasizes being intentional with *every* interaction that you have because they all matter. This includes being intentional in every place and way that you spend your time. You have to ensure that your vessel is always replenished because you want to be ready when people are clamoring for your services.

PRINCIPLE #4: CONTRIBUTION

"A tree is judged by the fruit it bears." – Parable of the Tree and its Fruits

July 2014 – NI recognized me for my company contributions

5 Principles to a Purposeful Life

A BURGER AND FRIES

My dad has been the pastor of the same Baptist church for almost thirty years. He's been preaching for just over thirty-six years. I've had a front row seat to watching him lead a church and community for my entire life. I owe much of my approach to leadership directly to being under his tutelage, but I can confidently say I learned way more from watching him work than I did from listening to him talk.

Once, we were returning home from his office, and there was a panhandler at the stoplight. He walked up to the car and asked my dad for "a couple dollars" to get some food. We could smell the stench of alcohol from this man. My dad replied, "How about I buy you some food. Meet me at the restaurant on the corner." We drove over to the restaurant and we went in with the man to buy him whatever he wanted to eat. My dad bought him enough food for him to eat right then as well as food for later.

The lesson I learned from him was that leadership wasn't about leading people to where they want to go, but rather leading them to where they need to go.

When my dad first arrived at his church, he was a young man with a vision of where he wanted to lead the church; however, he met resistance and realized he needed to make small changes that would move towards this vision as he provided the members time to adjust to a new leader. Like leadership, change is rarely easy and it must be done with intentionality. As time moved forward, he

seized opportunities to lead his

congregation towards where they needed

to go; eventually, the church membership

realized that where he was taking them

was for their own good.

Under his leadership as a pastor, the

church built a two-story annex and a

Family Life Center. All of this growth

opened the door for the church to better

serve the community. The congregation my

father served invested in him because he

demonstrated his leadership through

action.

MOSES

The summer before my freshman year, I participated in Mississippi State University's Summer Bridge Program. It was a month long program where high school participants took college courses for credit and gained exposure to college life.

I always think back to that time as a significant inflection point in my journey as it really shaped how I approached my college career. Many of the friendships that I have to this day trace back to my

experiences during the Summer Bridge
Program.

Because of my time at the Mississippi
School for Math and Science, I had already
completed the pre-calculus class that was
taught in the summer program. I also
never needed the extra time in study hall
to get help with my homework.
Unfortunately, study hall was mandatory so
I had to attend, even if I didn't have any
work to complete. It was in study hall that
I gained my first college nickname.

The lead mentor quickly grasped that I already knew the material that he would cover during the study hall, so instead of covering the material, he would allow me to lead the study session. Every time I entered the study hall he would call out, "Moses, come lead your people," while holding out the dry erase marker. That was his way of calling me to the front of the room to answer any questions and re-teach difficult concepts my peers did not understand.

At first, my peers were a bit reluctant to listen to my teaching because I was one of them. However, I consistently showed them that not only did I know the material, but I was excited about helping them understand it, too. I looked forward to study hall each day because it was my chance to take what I knew and give back to my friends. By program's end, I had been elected president of our class.

That month-long program led to me being involved and taking leadership roles in other campus organizations—fraternity president, senior resident assistant, and co-op ambassador. All of these occurrences required me to use my knowledge and actions to lead people to where they needed to go.

Looking back now, I can see the parallels between growing up with the opportunity to watch my dad's leadership, and my own leadership style. Even when you encounter opposition to your ideas or vision, as long as your intentions are pure and consistent, people will typically come around. Over time, I became better at casting an initial vision, and gaining the

support of those involved because

consistency in action was key.

THE UNBEATEN PATH

To work at NI in the ELP department, you have to have a degree in engineering (with the exception of chemical) or physics. There are a host of other qualifications, but your degree is important because ELP is the training ground for a future career in research and development, sales, or marketing. I didn't transition into any of them.

Instead, I started to seek out opportunities for roles in the training and development area. This extended my time in the ELP department, but because I used my time to exercise my leadership skills, I was able to move into a group who created, managed, and taught developmental training for the engineers selling NI's products. This became a continuation of me building on a career where I used my passion for developing others to make a tangible difference in a way that mattered to me. I went from leading teams and designing seller-focused training to working with a new department aimed at developing the entire company.

I can confidently say that my time at NI was instrumental to my growth because it allowed me to hone my skills and gain a better understanding of the principle of contribution. I entered NI in search of ways to combine my love for engineering with my love for helping people. I left NI knowing that my love for helping people is why I was placed on this earth, and engineering was just my pathway to my contribution.

Leading people to where they needed to go, and not where they wanted to go was possible because I consistently lived this mission every day. That same mission has led to this very moment with you reading this book, in hopes that this book will lead you to where you need to go. To do that, we must examine the principle of contribution in more detail.

DENDROLOGY

The principle of contribution states "a tree is judged by the fruit it bears." This is the same for you. You will be judged by what you contribute. You will, ultimately, be judged by what you do. Imagine that your life is similar to the parts of tree.

A tree's roots represent your core values; the trunk represents your principles; the branches represent different pathways you've taken in life; and the fruit that springs forth is the result of actions that you've taken. It is possible to produce both good fruit and rotten fruit. The quality of the fruit, what you contribute, hinges on your personal decisions. If you are uncertain of your values, then there will be inconsistency in your fruit.

Inconsistency is significant because when you're in a people-focused environment, no one will know what to expect from you. Any time you're led by values that just benefit you, your fruit will be rotten.

Understanding the power of the principle of contribution is vital because it directly impacts something we all care about: our reputation. People have no clue what type of person you are until they see or hear about the things that you have done. A reputation is built not only on the quality of your work, but also how you carry yourself. The very notion of a first impression is built on a list of things that people will subconsciously, or consciously, judge you on the very first time you introduce yourself. Items like a handshake, clothing, grooming, and posture are scrutinized during these initial encounters because they influence others' perception of you. Your first impression is the initial evaluation towards your core values because, when it comes to your reputation, people judge the entire package.

In a previous chapter, we talked about how in the business of you, every person that you come in contact with is a current customer or future prospect. Your reputation is the vehicle that carries your message to places long before you arrive.

You're actively crafting your reputation from the moment that you start a job, walk into a room, complete a

project, or interact with someone else, and

the principle of contribution is the tool that

helps you ensure your reputation is aligned

with where you're going. If this is the case,

why don't we just create a reputation that

everyone will love regardless if it's true or

not? I will answer your question with a

cautionary tale.

KITTENS MCGEE

When I teach my business' career development workshop, I often tell this story to illustrate a lesson I learned about the principle of contribution.

Kittens McGee is a kitten that self-identifies as a lion. Every time he pounces on a mouse, he does it with the ferocity of a lion. Because he is the biggest cat in his house, there is no one to question him on the validity of whether he's a lion or not.

As Kittens McGee goes throughout his day with his lion-like focus, the other cats start to talk. The cats start to spread the story of how Kittens McGee is a big, bad lion. This story spreads and eventually reaches the ears of Monkey Joe. Monkey Joe has been on the search for a lion because he has an actual lion encroaching on his territory. Monkey Joe was in need of someone to fend the lion off. Making an executive decision, Monkey Joe sends word that he needs Kittens McGee to come save him. Kittens McGee receives word that his services are needed and jumps at the opportunity to show this lion who's boss.

Kittens McGee shows up to Monkey Joe's house, and it's time for the showdown. Monkey Joe immediately realizes that he's in trouble. In one corner there is Kittens McGee and in the other corner there is an actual, living, breathing lion. What happens next is obvious—the lion eats Kittens McGee, Monkey Joe, and all of Monkey Joe's friends.

The story of Kittens McGee is sometimes hard to digest because we would like to believe that with self-confidence, and a little luck, we can overcome anything. However, Kittens McGee shows us that ensuring consistency in delivery and ability is about exploring your limits and understanding your blind spots.

Kittens McGee had opportunities to seek out bigger cats to see if his abilities were up to par; however, he was satisfied with just being the master in his immediate domain. It is vital that you place yourself in uncomfortable situations to stretch your talents and make intentional improvements. I'll give you an example of how I battled my inner Kittens McGee.

I talk to people for a living. Whether I'm teaching a class, giving a keynote speech, or coaching someone one-on-one, I'm talking to people. As such, I've long considered myself a decent communicator. However, a few years ago before Hawkins Development Group existed, I was terrible at networking with other people. I would attend a networking event and I would leave with zero business cards. I was leaving with zero business cards because people were consistently finding ways to end their conversation with me. I did not understand how I could have a successful one-hour coaching session with someone, but struggle maintaining a ten-minute conversation with a stranger.

To determine what I was doing wrong, I did what any self-respecting person would do: I went to more networking events.

Engaging in an activity when you know you're going to fail is about as uncomfortable as you can get, but I knew I needed to understand why this was a weakness of mine. I went into these events with the sole goal of looking for the moment when someone would get uncomfortable and start looking for an exit.

I found that roughly three minutes into the conversation, I started asking people penetrating questions about why they were motivated to engage in their professions, how their roles aligned with their purpose, and why they feel they were placed on earth. The responses varied from their eyes darting back and forth looking for an exit, taking a few steps backwards to create space, stumbling over their words, and excusing themselves to the restroom while never returning. What seemed like normal conversations to me were not appropriate to break the ice with someone I just met.

These are questions that I naturally want to know about people, so I can understand how I can help them reach their potential. But, there's a time, place, and pace for everything, and I had to reconsider including them in some settings.

Equipped with this knowledge, I could now set tangible goals to make improvements in this area. The next time I attended a networking event, I set a goal of talking to someone for five minutes without asking questions that had to do with purpose or passion. I met this goal, and eventually extended it to ten minutes, fifteen minutes, and soon could go a full conversation without ever asking those questions. I still wanted to know the answers to those questions, but I knew how to pace myself and save those questions for a second or third meeting.

By branching out and trying things, instead of just having the confidence that I can do them when needed, I was able to identify a blind spot and address it. It was important that I address this before I owned a business and needed to network for a living.

The moral of the story: to be consistent in your actions you must know your limits. Once you find those limits, set tangible goals to improve in those areas.

Be who you say you are, not what you

think other people want to hear. The

principle of contribution is about

authenticity, and your reputation should be

also.

THE REARVIEW MIRROR

Doubt is what poisons the fruit you produce. Doubt has the potential to kill your dreams before anyone else. Doubt is that little voice in the back of your head that asks, "*What gives you the right?*" when you have an idea for something new. Doubt is what causes you to act out of character because you're second-guessing your journey. Doubt is what disrupts your train of thought when arguing your point of view. Doubt is one of the fifty to seventy thousand thoughts that we have per day.

Doubt can only be defeated by the person in the mirror.

In many of the environments that I was in, I was the youngest, most inexperienced, or newest person in the room. Naturally, doubt was the first thing that would come to mind, but I quieted that voice by reminding myself of the things that led to me being in that room. If I was worthy enough to get to the room, I was worthy enough to be in the room. If a tree is judged by the fruit it bears, then I have every right to judge my own fruit.

Because I had made the effort to improve both my strengths and my weaknesses, I have every right to reflect back on what I've done as proof that I am who I say I am.

You have every right to reflect back on what you've done as proof that you are who you say you are. Being consistent in your actions is as equally important to other people as it is to yourself because in the darkest time, your consistency is your reminder of your capabilities. Your answer for dealing with doubt is in the mirror.

PRINCIPLE #5: MASTERY

"Always master your craft. Be so good at what you do, that other people will put their reputation on the line for you." – Larry Hawkins II

April 2014 – MS Gulf Coast Self-Branding Workshop

5 Principles to a Purposeful Life

WIND SPRINTS

Have you ever been to a little league game and saw the parent that's constantly yelling at everyone and everything? Thankfully, my parents never did *that*.

My dad was on the sideline coaching my basketball team while yelling at everyone to play better defense, crash the boards for the rebound, or in my case, stop traveling so much. On one hand, I enjoyed having my dad as coach because I was never late for practice. The downside to having my dad as a coach was that although he was tough on the team and wanted us to perfect the plays, he was twice as hard on me.

What I appreciated about having my dad as a coach is that he didn't yell, or make us exercise, re-run plays, etc. just for the sake of doing something. There was always a rationale behind everything he taught. One of his mantras was, "Practice doesn't make perfect. Correct practice makes perfect." We probably heard it at least three times a practice, and it became a staple of my childhood.

This saying was also applicable outside of the basketball gym. It easily translated because the intent of the saying was about mastering your craft. No matter whether it was sports, academics, friends, or video games it still applied. Having this expectation set at such a young age shaped how I approached everything that I did. I constantly searched for opportunities to hone whatever skills I wanted to develop so I would be ready for the big moment. This traced back to the number of extra wind sprints I had to run because of a lackadaisical effort at practice. I know I hated it at the time, but this is where the principle of mastery was born.

HATHORN HALL

I love listening to people talk. At MSMS, I had a big comfortable chair in my room where people would come to vent about their thoughts, problems, concerns, and dreams. I liked doing that so much that I found a way to do the same thing in college by becoming a resident assistant in Hathorn Hall on Mississippi State's campus.

My floor was filled with a mixture of freshmen and athletes. There were always problems that needed to be solved. Before

I could tackle those problems, I had to first learn about my residents. More often than not, I would hang out in my room with the door open to let them know that if they needed someone to talk to, I was there. I prided myself on being the most relatable resident assistant in the building. I learned as much about myself through my listening sessions as I did about my residents.

Because of my continuous effort to reach out to my residents and master my interpersonal communication, I was appointed to senior resident assistant the following year. With this appointment, not only was I responsible for my floor, but I was also responsible for resident assistants on other floors. Having spent the previous year perfecting techniques to help residents deal with their issues, I was equipped to coach my fellow resident assistants on how to deal with their residents. Practice didn't make perfect, correct practice made perfect.

KIT KATS

According to my records, I taught a version of my career development material forty-two times to five-hundred and sixty-eight people before co-founding Hawkins Development Group on January 1, 2014. That date was the culmination of years of practice and a series of big breaks. My first big break, covered in a previous chapter, came during that period of practice when I became a team leader during "Purpose Takes Root."

The second big break, referenced in "Sacrifice", came from teaching the material as part of the onboarding program. One of the stakeholders in that program was the ELP Training Manager. This manager was on an advisory board that was tasked with determining the agenda for the upcoming employee appreciation week. Unknown to me, during their planning meeting, the training manager recommended my class to be taught during the appreciation week.

After the meeting, the training

manager came to my desk to tell me about the decision and extended the offer to me. I had just been offered to teach my class on a company-wide scale for the first time, all because there was one person in the room who believed in me. She believed in me because I practiced. Not only did I practice, I practiced correctly.

I went on to offer a superb training class during employee appreciation week, and the Senior Learning and Development Manager decided to make my class a consistent companywide offering. Years

later, that same Learning and Development

Manager was instrumental in my seventh

big break. The principle of mastery is about

mastering your craft so that your journey is

a continuous series of big breaks. You can't

control how often the breaks come, but

you can control how often you practice.

FAIL FORWARD

Be so good at what you do that other people will put their reputation on the line for you. Don't be good just for yourself because that's not enough accountability. You're going to have days where you don't *feel* like it: the children kept you up last night, you haven't had your coffee yet, you're just not in the mood that day, or insert any reason that leads to you giving less than your all. That is unacceptable.

The principle of mastery often holds the most weight because it is the culmination of all the principles at once. The principle of mastery is about aligning your motivations with your purpose. The principle of mastery is about ingraining the betterment of others into your contribution. The principle of mastery is about fulfilling the promise that you're making to those around you about how you want to make a difference. The principle of mastery becomes bigger than you because not only is your reputation on the line, the person who recommended you has placed their reputation on the line too. If you were to fail, then *a lot* of people suffer.

You're going to fail. But, you want to fail in environments where the impact is much lower—this is why you practice. To this day, I still remember two of my most embarrassing failures that taught me valuable skills.

A few months into teaching the session across the ELP department, I held a class for roughly eight people. As I was talking about the rules for managing your

reputation, I discussed the danger of

creating a false reputation. It was within

this context that I used the word *façade*.

Except I pronounced it as "fa-kade." I kept

talking, but there were a few people in the

class who had a confused look on their

faces. As I searched my mind for what

went wrong, I instantly realized that I

pronounced the word wrong and I

corrected myself. After that event, I made

a conscious effort to use words I felt

comfortable with, and if I was unfamiliar

with them, I did my research before deploying them in a class setting. I thought I had resolved my diction issues. I was wrong.

As I mentioned in the beginning of the book, I was born and raised in southern Mississippi and had the accent to match. If you've never heard an accent from southern Mississippi, just know that we have the tendency to draw out the sounds of words unconsciously. During a workshop with one of our current clients, I found myself in a situation where I had to spell out my first name for an attendee. While watching the room, I said "L-A-arruh" and immediately a few of the students looked at me with puzzled expressions. I instantly knew what I said that caused the confusion so I started over, "L-A-arruh-arruh...." I found myself in a verbal loop of trying my best to just say "r." Roughly ten seconds later, I managed to say the letter "r" without drawing out the pronunciation, and the rest of the class went smoothly. This failure taught me about the importance of staying mindful of my accent so that I can remove any barriers that would prevent students from learning. It was another failure, true enough, but it was also a lesson that needed to be learned.

What I didn't know was that my path was going to take me places where I would be presenting to classes filled with students from all over the world. In these environments, reading the students' faces, using proper diction, and pacing appropriately were of the highest importance, and my previous failures enabled me to be highly effective in these new environments.

I failed multiple times on my journey, but learning from each event allowed me to fail forward. Without those failures, I would not have been adequately prepared for the opportunities that were on the horizon. Each of those opportunities, and many others, came from recommendations based on my capabilities at the time. By improving my skills, the quality of opportunities for which I was recommended improved also. Those improvements came equally from my successes and my failures, but only because I made sure to fail forward.

Mastering your craft enables you to have skills, talents, and a reputation that's worthy of being recommended. A word-of-mouth recommendation is one of the most powerful tools that will help you further your journey; however, you have to ensure you're worthy of being recommended. To

master your craft, you have to practice,

you have to fail, and you have to practice

again. Practice doesn't make perfect,

correct practice makes perfect.

CHALLENGE ACCEPTED

Growth comes from a place discomfort. This is why I continued to work with a client that I thought was beyond my capabilities. Each time I delivered a session, the results were good but not great. There was enough room for improvement that we both had a vested interest in making changes. Every time a date neared for the next event, I felt a sense of dread. I considered what excuse I could muster on why I couldn't teach this event, but I soon realized that I felt this way because I was uncomfortable. I had gotten into a routine with all my other sessions, and since this one was different it disrupted my standard routine.

It was in this moment that the principle of mastery kept me going. I could admit that with each session I taught, I learned a bit more about myself and what it meant to teach on that level. With each session I taught, it forced me to think outside the box in how I prepare and deliver my classes. With each session that I taught, I grew. Mastering a craft requires you to become excellent at areas where you have no experience.

The only way you can do this is by embracing challenging responsibility. I'm thankful for that client because he was invested in my purpose, and he knew I was capable of doing more than I saw in myself.

Reflecting back on the principle of contribution, if you're worthy enough to get into the room, you owe it to yourself to continuously improve yourself so that you stay there. To master your craft, you have to become comfortable with being uncomfortable if that is what it takes to stay in the room.

ICARUS

As you're mastering your craft, people will begin believing in your efforts and recommend you to others. It then becomes a precarious walk of pride versus focus on *why* you're doing what you're doing. This balance is aptly showcased by the story of Icarus from Greek mythology. Daedalus, Icarus' father, wanted to escape an unjust king so he constructed wings made of feathers and wax for himself and his son. Before flying away, Daedalus gave Icarus two rules: don't fly too low and don't fly too high. Icarus put on his wings and started to fly. Overcome with happiness from flying, he flew higher and higher towards the sun. In time, the wax melted and Icarus fell to his death in the ocean. Icarus represented the danger of pride, and for a brief moment, Icarus represented me too.

A few years ago, I was teaching a class to NI's ELP department. I usually start with a brief introduction; however, with this class, I spent the better part of the class talking about myself. It wasn't intentional, but it was as if I just couldn't stop myself. Later after the class, the attendees gave their feedback that said, *"The material was good, but I wish he had spent less time talking about himself."*

I was devastated. I had officially flown too close to the sun. I had done the exact thing that I was teaching not to do: placing yourself above making a positive impact on others. I immediately had to refocus my efforts. From that point on, I improved my message with each class taught. I made a deliberate effort to practice removing myself as the focus of the material so people would hear the actual message. The feedback on the class became less about me, and more about the material itself. The more I made it less about me, the more it was recommended to others.

Having others believe in you is an awesome confidence booster, but you must be wary of your pride. Their belief in you comes from your ability to take your passion, purpose, and talents and make a difference. Always keep this in mind, and be cognizant of not putting yourself above what you're able to do for others.

5 Principles to a Purposeful Life

THANK YOU

When I prepared to write this book, a friend challenged me to think about who I was writing this book for. She issued this challenge because keeping this in mind would help me articulate my journey in a way that truly mattered. The twist is that I wrote this book for everyone.

Purpose has no age requirement and it has no timeline. No matter where you are in your walk of life, I wrote this book for you. If you're reading this book, then

I've accomplished my mission. For that, I want to thank you. I am humbled that you took time to read about my journey, and I hope that it gives you what you need to continue your journey towards purpose. From the bottom of my heart, thank you.

ABOUT THE AUTHOR

Larry Hawkins II's life passion is inspiring others to pursue their purpose. An electrical engineer by degree, he has transitioned from optimizing electrical systems to helping others become the best version of themselves. Author of *5 Principles to a Purposeful Life*, *5 Principles to a Purposeful Life: Navigation Guide*, and CEO of Hawkins Development Group, LLC, he finds true fulfillment in helping people discover things about themselves that allow them to do more than they thought possible. As an author, speaker, and consultant, he has impacted thousands of people from around the globe.

CONTINUE YOUR JOURNEY

You have now completed book one of the *5 Principles to a Purposeful Life* book series. Personalize the lessons you've learned by working through the *5 Principles to a Purposeful Life: Navigation Guide*!

Available at www.HawkDG.com/store and www.amazon.com!

Made in the USA
Monee, IL
05 April 2021